MY BLOSSOMING EVERYTHING

MY BLOSSOMING EVERYTHING

PHILIP TERMAN

SADDLE ROAD PRESS

Saddle Road Press
Ithaca, New York
saddleroadpress.com

Designed by Don Mitchell
Cover painting by Christine Hood
Author photo by Greg Clary
Mercury image by Stephen Sykes / Alamy

ISBN 9798987954188
Library of Congress Control Number 2024903837

Also by Philip Terman

The Whole Mishpocha: New and Selected Jewish Poems
This Crazy Devotion
Our Portion: New and Selected Poems
The Torah Garden
Rabbis of the Air
Book of the Unbroken Days
The House of Sages
My Dear Friend Kafka (poems translated from the Arabic by Saleh Razzouk)
I am a Jew: A Holocaust Family Memoir (with Susan Terman)

For: Garden, New Star, Small Deer

Contents

What Is Poetry?

An indominable pulse deep down—
late last night I listened to an eighty-one-year-old
crazy about Whitman, yawping those lines
from the deepest wisdom inside his bones.

This morning, nine tomatoes ripening on the glass table,
two red, six various degrees of orange, one black,
a geranium potted on the porch rail, various birdsong:
robins, cardinals, the occasional towhee. Across

the road, cars pulling into the church driveway
for their weekly session with God. Cornstalks
tall as adequate basketball players. Apples
so abundant their branches bow down low

as if they were legs of dancers gesturing
their pliés. Eggplants basking on their vines
in the sun, and the onions just pulled
from their cozy bed. Thinking of the Yiddish proverb:

the little life inside the layers.
All of this from my perch on the porch.
The way the light plays with leaves
in a language I'd love to be learning.

August—the air dusking the garden,
the dog lazing in the shade of my chair
where I sit and compose these lines,
nothing dramatic, just staying awake

to the darting of the orange koi,
the indecipherable song across the water.
What's the word for when light dances
among the leaves of the hemlock,

the way fireflies—or do you call them
lightning bugs?—appear after summer dark?
Ok, then, get up, you weary thing,
and stop—right now—your sadness.

You are about to do something wonderful.

I

Every day of our life together
Ecclesiastes cancels a line of his book.

–Yehuda Amichai, translated by Stephen Mitchell

Written in a Blank Notebook
with the Torso of Mercury on the Cover

In this unlined empty notebook
you blessed me with when I had no other,

I will write only to you
until it is filled with my desire
as I filled myself up inside of you
mornings our bodies broke into waves.

Remember the lit candles?

Remember the spiritual music otherworldly
from the old radio?

     Remember the fire
against the harsh winter, and love?

Before it passes, before our memories fail,
as the corn leaves bowing into soil,
as the sunflower heads drooping, before

the seasons of the slow heartbeats
and the shocks, before the moment
our years frail like worn coats, and thin
into patches, let me say these words
into your ears

after some tired day of hands and eyes,
after you have informed the rooms
with all that you know—

     I apologize in advance
for my meager craftsmanship,
for my stuttering and my illegibility.

So bright we can read by them,

we said of the stars, the almost-full moon,
walking our routine around the gravel path
of the church and its cemetery.

Each night we rounded the dead.
What commandment were we observing?

And did those souls have some say-so in our circling?

Once our Jamaican friend swore the dead
stole into our living room and sat
at the table for a hand of cards.

You were grieving, she was your healer,
she saw this vision and said it was good,
that the dead feel comfortable here,
opening the windows, making small talk.

I said you were grieving.

That was in our other life,
which turned out wrong. Sometimes
you woke shaking and I tried
to hold you and keep you
in this world. It was that other life,
seeping through the floorboards

of your dreams. We couldn't
keep it out, not entirely, or mine,
with its rapid beginning and abrupt
endings, its unexplainable conclusions
and failures. We hushed those voices
with huge meals, and love after,

our one body crawling aimlessly on the floor,
our pleasure boat, in that hidden town,
that hilarious apartment,
how we understood time could stop a little while
if we became one person,

looking up suddenly at the first stars.

໒

We kissed during the last eclipse of the century.

The night was swallowing the full moon,
gobbling it up, slowly savoring,
or the moon was disappearing into its own dark.

We didn't know what all this had to do
with the planet's turning, its alignments
and laws. We were in the cemetery,
strolling, tired, the day sinking into sleep
like that moon into its dark ocean.

The century's last eclipse is saying something,
is saying who were the lovers who kissed
during the first and all those succeeding?

What is an eclipse after all but the blocking out
of light for another merging? Rilke said lovers
get in each other's way of their spiritual longing.

So why do I hear wings ferociously beating?

ॐ

All day I've been reading Isaiah,
who I imagine to be ordinary,
in love with a woman who like you

grows and then cooks the vegetables
and only cares about a happy life.
Ye shall be confounded for the gardens

that ye have chosen doesn't apply to her,
he meant it in a more rhetorical way.
And when he arrives home late, his voice

gone, his throat aching, feet scarred
and scratched from all the hard roads,
she puts in front of him a bowl

of last season's harvest: potatoes, tomatoes,
carrots, onions, basil, fennel, dill.
It tastes in his mouth not as the tongue

of fire devours the stubble
or *as the dry grasses sinketh down in the flame*
but more flavorful of their earth

than the live coals that touched his lips
and took away his iniquities. He loosens
the girdle of righteousness from his waist,

and takes off completely the girdle
of faithfulness from his loins,
being in any case more full

of the knowledge of his sources.
All flesh is grass, he whispers
into her ear, and the smell

of his fiery breath
makes her asks him to whisper it
again.

ॐ

We wear loose clothes, dancing in the kitchen

to the ancient radio with its bent antenna
directed toward the appropriate star—

sabbath evening slow-blues hour from Pittsburgh,
simmering with the chicken, onions, garlic—
two candles, the sourdough and wine—

what the scholars, who should know,
having studied the matter for centuries,
say is a foretaste of perfection.

All week we've stacked hay against the house,
gathered apples, put to bed the garden,
filling the feeders, cutting wood.

Tonight we eat an extra meal
and grow an extra soul for the other world,
which requires our presence

in the cardinal's flight out of the sweetgum
and in each folding of sky and in our clumsy waltzing
to John Lee and Muddy and Koko

before sundown as our departed ancestors
drape us in their holy dark.

჻

Here I do not attempt perfection—

only words that fall as now the snow
swirls and swoops through late morning,

accumulating without reason, each flake
falling into its own death,
white flecks of wind made visible.

We are each in our own room,
absorbed in our little pools of light.

All of this has the quality
of being unfinished,
we are still mostly in darkness,
ordinary and daily confusions.

All of this has the quality of mystery,
of something about to be revealed

or is itself a revelation.

჻

How to write each step
in each city we've walked—

the fruit stands, abandoned houses,
companion? Impossible

to detail the moments
in some logical pattern

the way we sauntered from
our pension to the Seine

that first night in the city
of light—3 AM and the squares

empty, the Eifel Tower blinking
through our talk. Or resting

on a patch of grass in Florence,
or on one of those benches

in the center of Broadway,
eating a knish, amazed

at the traffic of our good fortune.
I stare at this page and run

my hand through my hair,
Bach's cello tracing its rhythm.

Earlier we watched our world
fill up with snow. There's no

justification or rational in how
these moments steady themselves

and take on the form of a life.
Tolerance, forgiveness surely,

allowing each other our holy lonelinesses—
what does it mean to be a body

in a room it can no longer recognize?
When you forget the name you held

all your loving life on your tongue?

                                ∽

The way the earth washes your feet in soil—

I taste it on each toe, lick the callouses
hardening a little more each day
you walk your miles barefoot row
by row through broccoli and squash,
peppers and tomatoes, onions and cabbage
and pumpkins and basil—what

you can never wash off. So I have a little
of your garden in my lips, my tongue.

                                ∽

All the wisdom of the ages
has proclaimed the one truth
that one person is a completion
of another. Now the light divides
this small room in half and dawn
flickers at the edge of the trees
and a flock of swallows script
their one letter across the washed sky.
You have given me all this,

24

the wind sounding through the air
the urge of its own momentum.

જી

Study the torso on the cover
of this blank notebook you gave me.

The boy is without blemish
with his pure white marble
and his winged hat.

He is looking off to the side
to a place beyond the edges
and his fixed expression implies
that whatever he's gazing upon
is full of vision.

Note the sensuous muscles in his neck,
his shoulders, his perfect chest,
the contours of Adonis and Apollo
and the angels—Gabriel and Michael

and the ones in the German film:
Wings of Desire,
who couldn't resist becoming human,
wild and heavy with bad teeth
and always forgetting.

I wish these words were as perfect
as the boy's smooth cheeks
and nose and lips and eyes.

Even the fragment is perfect,
no rough edges—
he is complete in his ruin.

But already you have to struggle
to make out these homespun words,
squint your eyes, hold the pages to the light.

Note the cross-outs and starting-overs,
the awkward hand, whole pages ripped out.

Note how each letter is really a scribble
and scrawl of nonsense or
the nervousness of desire.

I'm saying the fingernails on the dresser
and the nubbins of hair in the sink
are flakes of me floating through the house.

This boy will never shave
or worry about clipping his toenails
in fear of accidently scratching his wife
during their supreme moment of bestial bliss.

I'm saying he will know no bestial bliss
for where the rest of his body should be is only air
or perhaps the ache of the amputated

or, as far as we know, the angels.

II

I'd rather live my life than not live it.

—James Wright

BEAUTIFUL BABY THING

Late May rains bursting the field
so tall our dog, charging towards
the pond, disappears into the timothy,
clover, ryegrass and who knows
what else. I've been wishing for Randy
with his tractor would hay the field by now,
the start, as far as I'm concerned,
of summer—ready as it is to be mowed
into the sweetest smell and bundled
and tied and dried and stored
for his horses and cows. But
he's got a day job and kids and, just
as we begin to despair into early
June, one night, late—the rain
stopped, finally—deep in sleep, we'll wake
to his engine and get up and look out
the window for the illumination
of his tractor lights blazing in a steady line
up and across and down and across
beneath the stars. But now we want
Randy to hold his horses in this after-
supper light of late spring as we trudge
through the field, our burleys misty
from the dusky dew—suddenly,
we stop in our tracks: what's that?
Barely visible, bedded down
in the soft mattress of the lofty grasses,
tiny, brown, curled up like a fetus,
spotted, still, delicate eyes closed,
and yes: it's breathing, this live
beautiful baby thing trusting us
to hold off the machine until its mother,

who our children's mother insists
is watching, determines: *it's time.*
It's time, little one. It's time to hobble up
and up on your slender legs and steady yourself
and run for your life.

WALKING

My first walk is also my first memory—

on the purple carpet, in the living room
of that bungalow in the suburbs built
for the soldiers who returned from the war.

One parent directed me towards the other
waiting with open arms,
both of them smiling, encouraging,

my brothers on the stairway cheering. No,

I don't recall if there was music playing
or if an uncle was filming that historic
occasion, I couldn't tell you anything
about the Cold War outside or how
the country was about to collide

with itself—you wouldn't ask me then
about what would become of us:

one parent's exploding heart,
the other parent's vanishing mind—

I don't even remember if I made it
to the other side without falling:

the only thing I can say with certainty
is that, between one parent and the other,

I somehow stood up and stumbled into my life.

ROBERTA ROSE

—remember those afternoons
when our mothers—Sylvia and Mildred—
took us out to Corky and Lenny's

for cinnamon toast and chocolate milk?
We were ten and lived five houses away.
I wish I could remember more—

how you were taller than me,
and wore your dark hair in a ponytail
and when my mother taught me to ride

my huffy banana seat I pedaled
to your house and up your driveway
and I got off my bike and you stood

on the front porch pretending
to pour tea into a plastic cup and I bowed
and kissed you on the cheek and got back

on my bike and rushed home.
Where are you now, Roberta Rose?
Does your cheek still recall my lips

the way a rose, after it's fallen
and become soil, recalls a spring dawn?
Let this poem be a rose, Roberta,

that I can present to you
for our lost childhoods, words
that disappear

into where our mothers sing.

AT CAMP WISE

At dusk I walk across the road
and beyond the church, the cemetery's
fallen leaves, the mowed field corn,
until I get to the edge of the woods,
and step a little into the woods.

Though I can't locate them, I hear
the shrieking choir of the blackbirds.

I first found out about death
at Camp Wise, after a ghostly bedtime story.
I couldn't fall asleep,

thinking about this new thing, this nothing,
myself ending, and everyone I knew
becoming no one,

and I began to sob,
quietly, afraid to waken the others.

I rose from the stiff cot,
tiptoed to the counselor's bunk,
whispered if he was awake, and now he was,
and he quickly dressed, old in his glasses—

and he walked me outside,
into the smell of trees, the dark—
damp, fresh, everything strange at this late hour,

and I asked:
Is it true?

And he, groggy: *yes, but not just you.*
All of us.
Even—he looked up—*the stars.*

And the screech of the blackbirds returns
my longing to carry everyone I love
for the rest of my life.

WHAT DOROTHY KNEW

Back in Kansas, mind
wakes before body, the sky
just paler than dark.

Muscles shiver,
as if from a field
of poppies, knowing

the fall into who I am,
one steady motion, a pulse
asleep to itself.

At the sink the cold
splash—the mirror shapes
its space for me: yes,

it was noble
what Dorothy did
for the cowardly lion—

taking him along
after he scared them
like that. Crouched

behind scowling trees
throwing apples,
I didn't know

what Dorothy knew—
how I could walk
right up to my fear

and slap it in the face.

TURN THE PAGE

Your best work is ahead of you,
my father said through the voice
of the medium, and I imagined

I would compose poems
I could only dream of, the book-length epic
that would finally interweave all my themes
into a grand synthesis, capping a career
of sputtering starts, approximations.

For surely my father, from his wider
perspective, would know the sweep
of time, though, in the flesh, what he said,
lying on the couch at the end of another
exhausted day at the used car lot, was:

If I see a story in a magazine
I might read it. But if I see a poem
I turn the page. I just turn the page.

And so now I wonder if what he meant
was that all of those words, even these,
all that sweat in a life almost as long

as his was, wasn't what he meant at all,
and that nothing I may have gained
from my chosen profession would match

the masterpiece that's assigned to me.

This Magnitude

Light-shimmering leaves branching
over the river—it doesn't matter

what one does or doesn't do today—
you can be relieved of your duties,

there's nothing more significant
than this stillness, this fragile surface,

this stained-glass airiness that will,
once you turn away, disappear into

where all the stories have retreated,
all the words and gestures exchanged

in all those moments you seemed
to be living in, with your loved ones,

all those incidents you don't remember,
stored, you want to believe, just behind

your left shoulder, or what was all
that spirit-work for, that labor, like trying

to carry water—those bodies you embraced
in body and mind, those hearts you held

in affection, all that attention you paid,
worth more than its weight—yet this grace,

the view of this afternoon river devouring
the flaming leaves, your being, you think,

too slight a thing for this magnitude—for now,
you can claim, for once, your life.

WILLIE WHEELER

My job's to wake them up.
6 AM dark, driving to the home
for mentally retarded youth—
crystals of snow on windshield
dissolve and are swept away: snow,
glass, sweep—you could lose
yourself in the steady falling
of cold stars sent from somewhere,
covering the landscape.

అ

Twelve years old, he's small as six.
Orphaned, anonymous: blue eyes,
like the boy Jesus, the nurse says.
I save him for last, after the others
are dressed and sitting cross-legged
on the floor, slowly rocking, eyes fixed
into a swirl of white dots on the set,
the way scientists stare for hours
into their secret sections of space.

అ

At his bedside, I try to follow
the blue lines that run crazy patterns
beneath his pale skin. I pull
softly at the cotton feet of his
baseball pajamas, but he keeps
on sleeping—seams of light steadily

whitening the frost on the windows—
keeps on sleeping, blond hair
on white pillow on the bed
he is strapped in, the way
gravity holds us in place.

My Brother and I Holding Hands

Is it such an uncommon thing?

It was just after our father died,
and we were driving
from the airport through downtown,

passing where he spent
his entire working days,
that long stretch of Carnegie Avenue
and all the way up Cedar Hill,

far as he made it in this life.

My brother's hand was just my size,
our fingers braiding each other's,
like bread,

hairy, like our father's, dark
and thick on the back of the wrist,
smooth at the knuckles, palms

seeping out each body's portion
of moisture, juices joined at the lifelines.

It didn't go anywhere, this new invention.

Was our father witnessing what our loss made us do?

How his absence brought this new
and determined animal into the world?

I Never Kissed My Brother

Or told him I loved him, no,

in all the years we shared
the same house, the same room,

maybe because we were boys-
turning-into-men, maybe

because it was assumed—oh,
yes, we joked, we laughed,

but we never talked about
the difficulties in that difficult

place outside the windows
and walls and beyond the yard

of 4073 Wyncote Road,
that world we never mentioned

but were nevertheless about
to enter, that world that would

change us into the people
we would become, that world

that would dare to ask:
did you ever kiss your brother?

On My 60ᵀᴴ Birthday

I rose in the still dark
and cold and put on
my father's army coat—
hanging in the closet
for years—*from the last*
Great War, he'd say,
the only one worthy
of the fight. I turned
toward the moon-
drenched field, the far pond,
warming my hands
in the pockets, wanting
not the emptiness I knew
but something I missed—
a scrap of paper scripted
in his familiar hand that
would reveal the secret
scrawled in the glory
of his youth, wise words
only he could reveal
and teach me how to encounter
this last phase of my life.
When he was my age,
he had seven years left.
They weren't lucky:
bad heart,
aggravation at work.
True to his generation,
he wasn't eloquent, only that
he was a sergeant and
he lost his two front teeth.
Daddy. What I still called him
in those few distant years

when we were men together.
Here he is again, full moon
mirrored in the water,
keeping me warm.

Decision: Second Child

On the day we finally decided to adopt our second child—

the dogwood blossomed its white petals,
the robin perched on its nest cupped between apple trees,

the enormous bees lingered outside the cabin window,
the frogs croaked in the majesty of morning,

the breeze picked up a little,
the clouds gathered in new formations that did not resemble
dragons or birds,

the house took on a deeper silence,
our first child did not quiver in her sleep.

III

Once for each thing, just once: no more. And we too,
just once. And never again. But to have been
this once, completely, even if only once:
to have been at one with the earth, seems beyond undoing.

—Rilke, translated by Stephen Mitchell

SPRING CHRONICLE

You say you want spring?
You say you've earned your daffodils,
your peepers, your swirling-wind song,
your sudden splash of light on the water?
You say the snow stayed you inside,
the ice broke you, the deep-freeze
pierced your marrows into sub-zeros?
You say your mind became unhinged.
You say that maybe you lost your faith
a little, in the bare feet in the soil,
in the later light, even in the trillium?
What do you say now? To the earth
softening? To the deep light of late afternoon?
What do you say to your quickening heartbeat?

ॐ

The garden strengthens hands—

Absorbing the soil,
the speared leaves of the lilac,
the corn up and out, the hyacinths
and roses overgrowing the arbor,
the strawberries safe from the squirrels—

Why look any deeper
than the garment of the moment?
No bible more beautiful than this—

my roost a woodpile,
my window a wide-open meadow
of fresh cut hay and wild flowers,

a robin nesting on the rose-vine
in its visible hour of budding.

የ

Spring morning brings its recklessness,
its flitterings and bird chatterings,
its newly sprung green promises.

You think you'll never say anything
again, and then this beauty arrives,
without conditions, save
your acknowledgement, walking through it,

praising this miracle of heartbeat
and breath after breath. How often

all this went on without you, how often
you cursed the inconsequential, desired
the ephemeral. Now it calls you out,

exposes and forgives, offers up,
no matter what, this birdsong.

የ

In spite of our sins,
spring is sprouting again—

the newly sprung leaves
of the blueberry bush don't
care about our concerns,
our fears, our issues, certainly

the robins are either unaware
or apathetic about our worry
about work or how we wander
aimlessly in the wider world.

Whatever, they signal,

continuing about their business,
hard-wired to the season,
an example for us all.

૭

May, mid-afternoon, spreading mulch
into the raspberry vines—
the cardinal's *pret-ty bird, pret-ty bird*—

or that's how its notes sound to us,
not experts in bird-speech, but
the song calls us to our tasks—

readying the garden, envisioning
our future harvest, though how
it will arrive at its imaginary abundance
will depend on our attention,

the everyday process of weeding
and watering, of keeping ears
and eyes to the weather,
of losing ourselves in our labor.

૭

Poet, I too can visualize
the school of orange-into-gold koi
swirling in the shadow of the pier.

And what do you make of the clouds'
designs under the surface? Do they,
too, speak of oncoming-rain?

No telling all we have in common,
you and I, you on one side of the veil
and me on the other.

Tell me: that thin-necked, pointed-beaked bird
landing silently and silently
flying off without so much as a farewell?
Was it a heron?

Or was it you again, with instructions?

NARCISSUS POETICUS

Years ago you planted these perennials for me
under their white arbor
between two shade gardens:

the *poet's daffodil*, proliferating
on schedule: mid-April,
so tiny, almost invisible, ignored
among—after the interminable freeze—
the sudden golden flourishing.

But just as beautiful—
miniature petals, stars-shaped
around the child's toy-teacup-sized crown.

The flower the famous God Nemesis
turned the beautiful boy—who could fall in love
only with himself—into.

Legendary as they are—
described by Theophrastus,
receiving a mention by Virgil,
named and labeled by no one less than Linnaeus—

they thrive—thanks to the early settlers—here:
"common," it is written, "in Pennsylvania." Particularly

in this blue vase you gathered them in
and placed on my desk
so their essential oils, resembling jasmine and hyacinth,
perfume my poems,

as you planned for them to do.

A POETRY AS PERFECT AS A JUNE EVENING

Hostas shimmering in the shade,
bush bursting with pink peonies,
robins flittering raised bed

to raised bed, the garden wet
with recent rain, the catbird
swooping onto the arbor. And

some say all we are is flesh
and blood and bones and the dust
and ashes that we become,

a name on a stone, insubstantial
as the air these songbirds sing
their hungers through. I giftwrap

this present and present it to you
and thus we sit in the cool soft air
and not feel so alone. Here we are,

together, all that my heart suggests,
all this longing bundled up like
that rosebud ready to burst,

flowering out to you who I trust
will nod and smile and understand
everything. It takes a lifetime

to get at the meaning of one poem,
or person, the other side of the moon,
a mystery without which we would be no one,

a dark water beneath the inscrutable
surface, rich soil out of which
these white Madonna lilies blossom.

So let's have a poetry as perfect
as this late June evening, the sun burning
down the several layers of the sky

and a mourning dove measuring
its five-note elegy. This evening—
daring me to say something worthy,

something that offers a small response
to this moment in all its grander,
but all I can manage are

a few words of witness—woodpecker
owning the apple tree, hydrangeas
absorbing the sharp light. We can sit

all the way through the evening and
not talk or read or even think,
we can hear the surrounding birds

and not assign names, or watch the slowly drifting
clouds without shaping them into
familiar figures. And the shadows across

the grass, no need to consider where
they begin or where they might end.
Simply to stroll out into the field

and lift ourselves onto a hay bale and observe,
from this rolled up bed of bound-up grass,
the epic of dusk turning into dark.

We strolled through it as it grew, quick
in the steady rain, and, when it finally dried,
listened as the farmer mowed and raked it

into windrows—we breathed in
the sweetness, turning ourselves
into summer, understanding

the dog, why, when we unfasten
her leash, she tears full-tilt across
the field, nose tracing the soil's

invisible scents, more alive than
we'll ever be, inhabiting the moment,
so deeply inside her body she takes flight.

And we call her name, call her name,
all the way down to the pond,
the lightshow of the fireflies,

the trees barely holding on
to their barely visible shapes,
the contours of the water dissolving,

the frogs' call-and-response
calming down all those daytime tensions,
croak after croak after croak.

And then the first star.

Our Ark

If it's the spruce it must be the mourning doves,
    if it's the willow—the two bluebirds,
    if it's the arborvitaes—robins

If it's the shagbark hickory—the red-headed woodpecker

If it's the red oak at the far end of the trail—
    the magnificent male pheasant

If it's the underbrush at the inflow-end of the pond—
    the woodcock

If it's the cattails beyond the outflow-end—the two geese

If it's the sweet Williams—it's the ruby-throated hummingbird

If it's the dark corner of the front porch—the spider webbing

If it's the barn rafter—the swallows

If it's the blossoming apple tree—surely the orioles

If it's the deep burrow near the basement—the chipmunk
    the attic—the squirrel (never the other way 'round)

If it's the pile of stacked maple—the possum we discovered
    in our headlights licking its paws, stock still, steadfast

If it's the recovering strip mine it's the blue heron
    and red-winged blackbird perched on cattails
    and pussy willows and at dusk the chorusing tree peepers

If it's the matted-down grass on the wood's edge—the deer

If it's the green shoots of lettuce—the slugs,
    the friendly snake in the squash patch

If it's the front porch rocking chair—it's the bull's skull
    and the cow's pelvic bone
    we arranged for our deranged still life

If it's the sweeping circle of the middle sky—
    it's the turkey buzzard or possibly the evasive eagle
    we saw once and once only perched on the roof
    of the abandoned house

If it's love we're making in the secluded field the other side
    of Sterret Road and the two blue silos—
    gotta' be the scurrying of wild turkeys

If it's the dream—it's the bear lumbering

MUCKING OUT THE SPRING

Every deep summer we traipse down to the spring
where we've designed an underground pipe
to divert a portion of the water through and into
our pond of koi and salamanders and tadpoles
and our sweaty bodies for some after-gardening
relief. Inflow, outflow, natural waters
the sages say we can be baptized in, waters
streaming into Wolf Creek become the Allegheny
become the Ohio become the Mississippi—now,
the spring is clogged with leaves and limbs
and who knows what litter decayed into a thick
black mud-like goo we have to scoop with our hands
out of what has seeped through cracks and fissures,
numbing our fingers that reach deeper for the humus
and hurl it onto the bank, the slime staining
our hands and these old clothes we wear for the purpose:
to release the flow so our waters may rise again.

SNAPDRAGONS FOR VAN GOGH

Color of finches in flight,
unobtrusive as finches

concealed in the upper stories
of the spruces. Shaped like bells

or summer skirts, this season
just before the sunflowers

crown their slender stalks.
In France we walked along a field

of sunflowers reaching
beyond the afternoon's borders,

a whole city of them.
We didn't know each other well

so we paused awhile
in front of Van Gogh's grave,

buried beside his brother,
strewn with sunflowers,

this final acknowledgement
that though he lived a poor life

and lonely what he taught us to see
can return even if it is only to

the decayed flesh and bones of him.
The snapdragons are more yellow

than the light that fills this room
with its walls of windows and floor

of fresh oak and ceiling of skylights
so that as much of the day can move

as much as possible through it.
Who wouldn't bring in the outside

if they could? Your hands are yellow
with the stains of them. If Van Gogh

painted snapdragons they'd resemble
fire, flames out of the dragons' mouths.

Now it is easy to miss them
in the sun's glare. You pick a vase-full

and place them beside me, offering
a little more of the garden into the house.

GOLDENROD HEARTS

Like sunrise
on the far side of the pond,
their spikey blossoms
break the heart, color
of the necessary school bus
that too soon will pause and slide
its heavy door at the corner
of Mill and Scrubgrass Roads
and close. Bella and I tossed the football
as we waited, the wildflower
a wet yellow in the blinding sun
as it rose inside us,
its bright gold filled with nectar.

All parts of the plant are safe to touch.

Not to be confused
with the inconspicuous ragweed.

Golden: to remind us of what's left
of summer; rod: for Aaron,
who cast it down
and it become a snake that swallowed
the magicians' snakes, and so:

it put forth buds,
and produced blossoms.

Wildflower of good fortune,
wildflower of pioneering spirit,
wildflower signaling, each year,
for us to capture

what's left of paradise while we can.

FLOCK

I hope you love birds too. It is economical. It saves going to heaven.
   —Emily Dickinson

1.   *Appointment with the Peacocks*

Eeyawwk, eeyawwk—
we open the car door window
to their weird chant,
distinctive and piercing
as they spring back
to the spring house,
dart up into dark spruces
in their brilliant bodies,
an impossible blue-green,
as if light shone from inside
out. We bear gifts
in the form of bread we tear
and toss in the direction
they skitter towards, shy
and nervous, snapping
the brown crumbs then backing
away, not greedy or gracious—
reserved rather, unconscious
of their obvious beauty
and the arrogance
of their appearance, their walk
a strut as they circle
the blueberry bushes
in their luminary regalia,
unaware, like children,
of the attention they call
to their display. Against
such color the sky, the geese,
the horse, the field, our skins

disappear. We watch
all evening until they retire
into the dark tops of branches.
I can stare at this one,
who lingers, until I arrive
back to its source, to India,
or to that place where blue
was created until,
in response to my longing,
it flowers its train as if
I'm the one he's attracting,
and I'm lost in dozens of eyes
staring back at me, each
refuting everything I knew
about the exotic.
Briefly he pauses in all
his iridescent glory,
where the daylight has gathered.

2.   *The Pigeon*

landed in the garden
one spring afternoon
as we were mulching
and planting seeds—

small and alone and lost
in the center of all that soil,
stumbling, withdrawn.
We slowly approached—

yes, we've seen thousands
but up close? The black stripes
around the slate grey feathers?
The fluorescent green neck?

The white heart-shaped
cere on the beak,
the delicate slanted oval eyes,
the soft head, the two

blue tags around each
thin-as-a-twig leg?
It hobbled into the grass.
We approached closer to read

the numbers on the bands
and googled the racing club
it belonged to, called the owner
all the way in Buffalo,

200 miles off-course.
Trained to brave the weather,
predators, electric lines, hunters.
We secured arrangements.

It wasn't difficult to tease it
into our chipmunk trap, set it
gently on the front porch
beside a cup of water, some seeds,

until the owner arrived.
It stood there, stock-still,
eyes glazed, exhausted, as if
it never wanted to fly again.

3.   *Swallows*

We discovered them by accident,
in the complicated
architecture of their nest,
a bristled upside-down skullcap

or crown of thorns,
fixed as if permanently
to the rafter in the shadowed
corner of the barn
like a sculpture in bas-relief—
mud and straw
and twigs and doghair—
more secured to their board
than the hardwood itself
is to the beam. Inside,
four, just-hatched, tiny
as our pinkies' finger-
nails, still clinging
to bits of their broken shells,
down moist from the other world.
In a Soho gallery
It would be called *naïve*
and prominently featured
in a showcase labeled:
Artist unknown. Materials:
Northwest Pennsylvania,
tagged well beyond
the means of the middle class.
Each day, between rototilling
and fixing the lawn tractor
and looking for the proper hoe,
we would stand tiptoe
on the mud floor and peer
into their private place.
They'd curl around each other
into a center like one
pulsing animal. Counting
each additional feather,
we noticed the stubs
of wing bones and knew

they would soon be gone.
We had to call them fledglings now,
stacked like ornaments one
on top of the other, framed
against the slivers of June sky
visible through the slats,
staring up at us with eyes
black as dark wells.
Their mother allowed
those few moments of silence
before squawking us away.
One dusk they one by one
flew straight at us,
their transgressors, into the emptiness.

4.   *The Flying Squirrels*

Strange, nocturnal sounds—
frozen January, time to fill
the feeders. Opening the shed door,

something—a chipmunk?—darting
from wall to wall, spreading out
what looked like bat wings,

staring back at me
with huge bug eyes as if
I was the intruder.

I slammed the door once, twice,
in hopes to scare it back out,
but no, it's happy with this shelter

and the plastic bag of birdseed
it ripped open and scattered across
the green tarp lining the wooden floor.

I considered the diminishing
number of cardinals, woodpeckers,
mourning doves pecking

not so patiently at the white ground,
waiting for their order to arrive.
Opening the door again, slowly, stepping back,

peeking into the dark cavern—
in the far corner, a small bowl of shredded bark
and dry leaves, balanced on the hemlock board,

the tan fury thing beside it—
and another of the same kind flung out
and I flung back, thinking rabies,

and—who knows?—typhus,
rodents swarming in my sleep.
Didn't I read, once: *endangered,*

a priority species, protected—
prefers old growth forests, conifers?
They cluster to keep warm.

What about the live trap,
fill it with seed? Haul them,
one at a time, into the woods where

they can carry on their love affair
and dreams for the future
and we could lure back

our multi-colored birds,
reseal the cracks in the shed?
This morning, checking

the trap, locked in—curled up—which one?—
in the corner of the cage—
innocuous, a child's toy, eyes open.

Buried it in the woods.
Laid branches over its tiny body.
Returned the trap back to the barn.

Thought about the other.
Gliding like a ghost.

5.   *Where the Ducks Walk on the Fish*
            The Spillway in Linesville, PA

Not as miraculous as Jesus
strolling on the surface, but

still, we travel great distances
for the rare vision of these creatures

assembling from their separate elements
as if by appointment—

the ducks swimming across their sky,
the carp flying through their water.

How each long to be the other—

the ducks dreaming of carp,
the carp dreaming of ducks,

how we yearn to fuse into what
we are not, to submerge

into that mystery, that dream-life,
taking the strangeness into ourselves

and changing us, the way these ducks
swoop down onto the runway of these carp,

the way these carp lift themselves
almost out of their water to prop up these ducks,

each surging toward the other
out of some lack or hunger for the bread

tossed from the bridge above them.

6.   *Child of God*
            for Curt Yehnert

We were drawn by the starlings
who dropped their waste
over everyone's head

but nevertheless flew
through the crazy air
to their own kind

a little later each evening
and filled maple and elm
like purple leaves, sounding

the ember dusk, those
thousands of nuisances.
March, late afternoon,

half-blue, half-orange sky,
small patches of snow
still melting

into the shadowed lawns,
our false spring
before the final blizzard.

In the temporary warmth
we cut class, pitched
pennies against the Church

of the Assumption The way
you guided a pinball
to just that spot of flipper,

you followed your coin
as it spun
within an inch

of the transubstantiation.
I know what it's like here,
you said, pointing to the wall:

*I want to know what it's like
there: a true child of God,
your eyes so wide with belief*

you were half-way already.
Now,
the man the man with his science says

it's all biochemical
and nothing can save you,
not even the lithium. Soon,

the concentration will go little
by little into the other world.
After dark the authorities

blasted them out,
over our heads wings
pulsating with their smaller explosions.

7.   *Under the Flyway*

Less grinding than a truck, more of a roaring than a rumbling,
an ascending—fainter, fading into inaudibility, somewhere
into the silence out of which it came. An ethereal railroad, an
atmospheric migration route, a highway of the air. Long white
strands of vapor trails, chalk lines, dividing the sky into its
own delineations, crisscrossing clouds, looking like the stuff of
clouds, though vertical, stretching out like banners. An invisible
hand pulling a long string. All afternoon you can watch it slowly
recombine back into the elements. Between airports, we measure
hours by flights, the celestial traffic. In this rural pocket, we're
alone but dozens of citizens trespass over us, our airy neighbors.
We're where they look out from the safety of sealed windows—at
our tiny houses, our fields and farms, our dirt roads intersecting
at right angles. Those figures in gardens, on porch swings: that's
us, we're those dots disappearing into oblivion. We're where
they're looking when they glance away from puzzles and thick
novels until we become as indistinguishable to them as they are
to us. Invisible, these borders dividing one country from another.
Travelers look down and wonder: what town? Municipalities
become inseparable from the land surrounding. We fade into
the earthly mass. We go about our tasks. The water's boiling.
Beep goes the microwave. The rabbits are ruining the lettuce. My
daughter points her finger heavenward: there it is. Where from?
Where going? Immeasurable miles of unmitigated space. My
daughter likes to fly. I lift her horizontally, she flaps her arms.
Where is she floating? Some say they fly in their dreams, where
they lift themselves above their daily toils. We fill feeders so we
can watch birds swoop and soar. What do the koi think of the
heron? Water lilies of starlings? A plane recalls us to its moment.
Take two steps back. Squint into its disappearance. Return to
our only world.

To a Blossoming Apple Tree

Don't tell me Isaiah was clear-headed,
that he had it planned out in advance

when he ordered us to turn our swords
into plowshares.

Don't tell me Jesus spent weeks drafting
that mountain sermon song.

That robin isn't studying any lexicon.
How long can we follow the movements of the bee

as it chases its hunger from apple blossom
to apple blossom, white and pink petals spinning

onto the field spread with mustard seed
and coltsfoot? And these words?

Can they offer an approximate portion
of their sweetness like these messages that float

and land on my notebook?
And so I strategize how to preserve them,

in this soft breeze, these swaying shadows,
these singing robins, that lone goose sneaking

through the stubble far from its natural waters,
in just this mid-morning light, under just this sky's blue clarity,

ignoring, for now, the impossibilities,
the tragedy of the next page, the indecipherable hour,

the shadows lengthening, the air warming,
late morning evolving into early afternoon,

the wind brushing the fallen blossoms across
the shadow of the tree they floated from.

So what else to do with all this time
than to sit under this blossoming apple tree

and try to blossom myself?

A Million Angels Falling

But how else can we live,
if not in the upper story of this abandoned loft,
where we've been assigned to alert the town
        of the precise moments the rain turns into snow?

And when was the last time you sat before a window
and did nothing
but watch the all-day accumulation?

Wasn't it when you were a child,
still in your pajamas, school cancelled,
your whole life opening like those flakes swirling
        beyond your reach?

Now the snow is exhausting us,
but is nevertheless beautiful.

Sometimes I don't want to follow the story.

I want to wander across the page like my scattered
        thoughts that involve memory and desire and are random
        and we have nowhere to be and nothing to do
        and no one's death to grieve,
        not even our own.

And still it snows and I write to some rhythm my ancestors
        suggested in the dark regions of that other world.

We look out into the snow for answers
        and discover our happiness, which we accept—
we trust the architectural silence of each flake
        as they draw their abstract visions on the air.

We return to the established texts,
these morning-into-afternoon-into evening pleasures.

We can call it a curse
or we can call it a blessing—
it dares us to observe how it piles up.

It wants to show our hearts are a million angels falling.

Turn inward, it says—

the day is ours, stay inside and use all these extra hours—
we have so few—for loving,
these hours that, after we die, we'll die to retrieve.

The snow is silence's signature.
It's writing a poem
it erases and revises to write another, and another.

Our daughter stares out the window into her future memory—
great storm, school cancelled, anything possible,
smell of cookstove smoke, sleep lingering in her hair.

If she could capture a flake on her stuck-out tongue...
If she can see to the other side of the snow into summer...

She can sit on the stairway all day alone
following it fall into her mother's garden.

A Staying

Now is the time for strawberries—

our daughters pick all they can,
save the ones noshed by the chipmunks,
save the ones claimed by the slugs.

᭞

Peretz Markish:

> I would embrace all the cows
> and stretch out with them on the earth
> and howl together.

᭞

We light a candle for the dogwood,
anticipate the hydrangeas,
are content with the hyacinth.

᭞

Yehuda Halevi:

> Sweet would be onto my soul
> to walk naked and barefoot upon the desolate ruin
> where the holiest dwellings are.

&

Here, on a summer morning,
the garden pulsing toward
its full fruition, it's easy to mistake
the vestibule for the banquet hall.

&

Izzi Charnik:

> *Who cares if eternity won't know me?*
> *if no one watches my footsteps.*
> *But right now, when hearts are burning,*
> *I must come with my song!*

&

Now is the time for the cutting of hay
and the sweet walks down Mill Road,
for the turning of the earth
for sorghum, clover, field corn.

&

Aleph Katz:

> *Better to live this way,*
> *a lone thorn in the field*
> *than the golden way of the world*
> *that charges a quick death*
> *for its straw, its bread.*

❦

Just this, just this, a perfect June evening—
stillness and birdsong, the garden just tilled
and the evening primroses yellowing their trumpets
towards the disappearing light and now
a hummingbird in the morning glories
and the air a softness and just the right
degree of coolness and you approaching
with a blue water can and the mourning dove.

❦

Anonymous:

Who wouldn't want a heart transformed into a hummingbird?

❦

It's all a staying, griefs
and your beloved dead allow you
this seat by the garden, these moments
as if you've passed through a curtain.

❦

Isaiah:

Cease to do evil.
Learn to do well.

&

Consider your inheritance,
how your ancestors were prophets
of the holy throne,
trudging through the desert,
chasing a book.

&

Yehuda Amichai:

> *Through the wound in my chest*
> *God peers into the universe.*

&

Reverence is not so slight a word
for those two fawns leaping
across the clover field into the dark
woods.

I was distracted.
I was lost in a knotted place.

I happened to have looked up.

And there they were.

&

Eli Wiesel:

> *I order you to shake your sadness away.*

❦

And so:

Out of fashion as this poem will be,
this poem of ecstasy and service,
this document of summer,
days of drought and resurrection—

❦

The sunflower seeds
    return to the nuthatch,

the butterfly bush flowers
    call the butterflies,

the apple trees remind the orioles,
    the sweet Williams pause for the hummingbirds,

and your half-turned figure
    returns me to you.

IV

All the new thinking is about loss.
In this it resembles all the old thinking.

—Robert Hass

The Poetry

For Deanne Goodwin

In the café in Franklin, Pennsylvania,
a poet was dying. I didn't know what
to do for him, save to listen to his poem

he recited in a gravelly voice,
half-a-lung gone, the cancer already
in his liver and neck, the lymph nodes

so swollen they had to knock him on his ass
with chemo to perform surgery and even
then they're not certain. "4th stage,"

he manages. We're in a circle, before the fire.
"5% chance of living 5 years."
We move in closer to his voice,

huddle around his poem. Deane,
that was the last time I saw you
and you knew you were dying because

you told us it went to the brain
and this time, when you rarely
spoke—if at all, unless asked—

about what you had already out-
lasted, we knew it, too.
We sat in that book-lined room,

talking about what we loved most
—you and I argued, oh, yes,
we heated up about formal

versus free verse and how what
I would say in a lot you could say
in a little, big man, delicately

crafted word-jewels surrounded
by delicately crafted silence.
And naturally the very last

I heard from you was your voice
tonguing words that took you
all your life to write: "Children leap

summer/for youthful joy of movement,/
do you remember?" in a voice I can only describe
as biblical water, the calm kind

that someone could cross over.
Deanne, I told you I would call
and I didn't and it was too late.

You were the poetry.

The Mourner

Walking my dog in the cemetery
across the road and there he is again—

car parked at the edge of the woods,
sitting in his folded chair, listening

to country music from the transistor radio
he'd placed on top of the pink granite

sculpted into two hearts, one for her,
one for him. Between their names—

an open locket: both smiling, she's
leaning her body into his body.

Set atop the grave: chrysanthemums,
roses in black vases, six solar lights, a statue

of Jesus, a metal pumpkin. A wind-
chime and a heart with an arrow

on the maple tree's branches
where he hangs lights and decorations.

He shovels a path at Christmas.
He keeps steady hours—

sunrise, mid-afternoon, after dusk,
told us he'd be joining her soon.

Once, we heard a gun blast. We rushed
to the grave, but there he was, meditating.

He placed a cellphone in her casket
in case of resurrection.

We'd like to tell him
to leave the dead alone, to return

to his daily tasks, we neighbors
are concerned about this crazy devotion.

But there he still is, New Year's Eve,
waiting in his car in the oncoming dark,

keeping his companion company,
as if his attention wavered,

she will leave him alone for good.

THIS ABSENCE

Are you jealous of me, brother,
eating this apple in the sun

at my window overlooking
the water, my two children

playing dress-up, my wife
readying dinner? Do you wish

we could exchange places,
you and I? You would

take on my flesh, and I
would descend into your dust,

perhaps for a day, an hour,
an instant? Or do I have it

all wrong, and you wouldn't
trade places with me for all

the world? That even
the fires of the flesh are nothing

in the silent reaches
of where you are, and perhaps

I should I envy you, that light
you've become? And perhaps

my life is really for you
a death, and your death

another life without this apple,
this water, this absence?

LOST DOG

The neighbor girl calls out for her dog,
missing since last night, her voice echoing
its lamentation across the valley separating

her grief from ours. Mid-March, the sun
registers itself, as if the union
for which it operates has finally resolved

its endless negotiations with the clouds.
Sand-y, Sandy-y, the girl sings its two-note
rhythm. Ice thins into the pond's surface.

We lost one once:
I was just this neighbor girl's age: ten.
Blackie, his name. I'd be first to rise

so I could pet him all I wanted and still
he wanted more. Once he followed me
to school and the teacher gave us both

the rest of the day off. One evening
he didn't come home, just like that,
and after the search and the giving up

I thought I saw him. Up all night, glued
to the window that overlooked the street,
the faint last dark indistinguishable

from the faint first light. He streaked,
a black blur, across the suburban lawns.
I woke my father but I still don't know

if it was him or if it was my heart shaped like him.
Now she approaches. *Have you seen her?*
Sandy? Face puffed, as if she'll never know

another night of complete sleep again.

THE RABBI OF BOX TURTLES

For Dr. Bill Belzer

Bill, at first I mistook you for a Chassid—
flowing bushy beard, tall, lanky
and—yes, you were a rabbi of sorts,

a Talmudic box-turtle expert. Like Moses,
they can live up to 120 years but in the wild,
a small parcel of woods where they hatch,

eat slugs, worms, berries, lay their eggs,
biologists like you just beginning
to understand the delicate population

dynamics. You knew they were dying out—
pet collectors: *Leave them be!* you repeated,
your mantra, a box turtle yourself,

a self-described "isolate," hiding out
in your corner office on campus,
eating your peanut butter sandwiches.

You knew it was we humans who ruined
them, our penchant to gather and hold onto
and collect, no matter the repercussions.

But it took you to propose the project
of using perpetual radiotelemetric retrieval
to monitor and protect and possibly rebuild

the "extirpated Box Turtle population."
Belzer's Protocol, they called it—signaling
to all the lost through captivity and injury

and habitat destruction that they can be monitored—
radio transmitter attached to their shells—
their movements followed. They can, like children,

be parented, the congregation you nurtured,
made certain they didn't wander off too far,
their nests well-leafed, attended to if wounded.

You created an endowment in perpetuity
that would follow the death of the project's
originator—yours, Bill, more than a year ago,

I just learned from a colleague. You told her
not to tell anyone about the brain tumor,
your decision not to pursue treatment: 70,

you made your decision like a scientist
or like Rabbi Hillel—you understood you are not obliged
to complete the work, but neither are you free

to desist. And so the box turtle commandments
you adhered to and thus wrote down:
Leave it untouched! Behold a life form

that graced this earth before and long after the dinosaurs!
Spread the word to children everywhere—
scout groups, classrooms, bedtime stories!

Naturally, your burial was green.

When the Syrian Human Rights Worker

began to speak calmly and slowly
of his prison experience,

a girl sitting beside me
was consulting her cell phone.

During his story about his arrest,
I noticed she was scrolling Facebook.

As he was describing how, one
by one, his nails were tweezered out,

she was composing a text.
When he developed the part about the quivering

of his body from electric shocks,
I tried not to look down

at the smiling face emoticon
she included before pressing *send*.

When his eyes shut as if reliving the moment
and whispered: *they hanged me by my hands and legs*

and tried to split me in half—
a showtune sounded from my jacket pocket.

This poem was written by Nasser Rabah, who lives in Gaza, which is currently being bombed by the Israeli Army in retaliation for Hamas' brutal attack on Israeli citizens, killing 1200 and taking 236 hostages on October 7, 2023. To date (January 1, 2024), over 20, 000 Gazans have died in the war, including over 8000 children. The poem was translated from the Arabic by Saleh Razzouk with assistance from Philip Terman. When Nasser wrote the poem, the number of children killed was 4000. Most tragically, the title would be changed daily.

4000

Dec. 1, 2023

Four thousand,
Four thousand,
Four thousand.
Not four, not forty, not four hundred.
Four thousand soft hands touching right now the gate of Allah.
A chain of little angels covering the sky of this life.
Life looks old without children.
Four thousand lost kisses staggering in the air,
Four thousand white butterflies without flowers to land on,
Four thousand times the word: "Mama" will not be said.
Four thousand times the word: "Papa" will shatter
        the heart each morning and evening,
Four thousand colorful shoes tucked under empty beds,
Four thousand school bags guarding the sorrow of homes,
Four thousand morning sandwiches left on tables
        that no one will reach for.
Four thousand broken bicycles abandoned on the roads,
Four thousand one would not enter the school door,
And will not attend graduation ceremonies,
Would not buy Eid clothes,
Yet will be with no friends.
Nobody could ask about their wishes when they grow up,
Sitting forever next to a river of tears.

Four thousand photos on the walls,
In four thousand fathers' pockets sipping grief.
Starving sparrows on four thousand mothers' windows
        pecking the heart's bread.
Four thousand scents that won't leave their pillows,
Four thousand books gathering the dust of longing,
Four thousand eternal laughs breaking the glass of time.
They will not grow older, will not depart from the last scene,
Will not flee the rubbles,
Will not find an ambulance,
Will not make it to a hospital,
No mourners escorting them to funerals,
No flowers on their graves.
Only four thousand on the news.

SOME OF THE CHILDREN

This girl's neck wrapped in a Palestinian scarf.

This boy wearing a yellow sweater,

This boy's hair combed unevenly across his forehead,

This boy is wearing a red short sleeved pullover shirt,
    his body turned to the side, his chin resting on an arm,
    his face wearing a mischievous grin.

This boy's hair is meticulous, his neat white shirt buttoned
    to the collar, under a formal black jacket,
    he is the classiest one, and I bet he's thoughtful and kind.

This girl's face is larger than the frame can hold—a close up:
    rosy cheeks, a few inches from the photographer.
    This baby is still crawling.

This girl's white hijab is wrapped around her whole face,
    her smile total in its completeness,

But that is true for all of them:

This girl wearing a tierra,

This boy wearing the sunglasses sliding down his nose
    over a smirk like he just did something really cool,

Even the three children wearing the pandemic masks,

This boy with his hairstyle in a pompadour, Hollywood
    handsome, modest eyes staring slightly downward,

This boy whose hair is parted to the side and combed
across the forehead the way my mother combed mine
mornings before grade school,

This tiny girl wearing her pink sweater, hair in pigtails,

These two—brother and sister—in one frame—you can tell
by their silliness, staring playfully at each other—

This girl who knows exactly who she is, her hijab wrapped
tightly around her head, a light blue and decorated
with bright stars that glow.

RIVER OF MANY NAMES

1. Our Rivers, Our Lives

We raft down our rivers:
Tuppeek-hanne, River of Hate, Clarion,

following the waters through the currents
of our days, swimming on their surfaces,
losing ourselves in their depths.

We could fish until we grow old
or simply stare like we were wise
and gather together the experiences
of our many selves.

We could pray in droughts for its rising,
in floods for its holding back.

We could baptize our bodies
and come out a new religion.

2. Above Five Forks

For ten good minutes the eagle
threads the air above the river,
appearing out of its famous nest
behind your left shoulder. It glides
in wide circles, white head, black
outspreading wings, owning its own
pocket of sky, allowing us time
to fool with binoculars, only
to abandon them in favor
of our naked eyes. We hiked
this far on the first real day of spring

to explore the wilderness and ourselves.
The sun flares the full leaves on the far bank to fire.

3. *Lower Two-Mile Run*

We took off our clothes
in the sweat of the July
afternoon and, avoiding
the sharp stones and glass
chips, toed the scum
settling on the surface, and
I wondered about the chemicals
from the refinery, but you spoke
of trout spawning up the creek.

4. *Clarion River Chronicle*

The Indians called you Tuppeek-hanne,

The French called you—who knows why—River of Hate.

Pioneers called you Tobeco and Stump Creek.

State surveyors, camping along your bank, heard,
    through the silvery spray, your distant ripples,
    like soft trumpets, as if calling them to a service,
    and called you *Clarion*.

River of many names, stream that flows from a large spring,
    your sound was the music they heard in 1817,

the steady green murmur beyond virgin pine, deer, elk,
    bear, wolf, panther, wild turkey.

From the East Branch to the Allegheny, the spine of the county,
let's imagine you before the bituminous coal dust stripped spaces
    of land,

before Thomas Watson in 1810 drilled a salt-well near
    the mouth of Deer Creek, and struck oil,
    what the Seneca used for paint and medicine, and—

as the chief recited the conquests and heroism of their ancestors—
    what the tribe would gather on the surface and torch
    into flames, their shouts and songs echoing off
    the surrounding hills,

before the first of thirty-one furnaces blasted the water
    of Little Toby Creek, half-stacks of rough stone,
    dressed at the edges, burning charcoal, exhausting the timber,
    deforesting the hemlock and pine, transported downstream
    to the Allegheny, then the Ohio, then the Mississippi—

Those were the halcyon days, claims the writer of the chronicle,
    meaning workmen with wages, economic boom
    in iron county,

before Christian Frederick Post, the first white man to cross,
    circa 1758, wrote: "we crossed the big river Tobeco
    between two mountains,"

before the government of Pennsylvania extinguished
    the last claim of the Indians by purchasing the land
    with deeds, treaties,

before Alexander Moorhead, mighty hunter, in what is called
    a "picturesque tale," bet an Indian on who would kill
    a deer first and, as a stag approached Cherry Run,
    he leveled his rifle at the red man, shot him dead,
    then killed the deer,

before another Indian, Jack Snow, camped on your creeks
    and a white man—the storyteller won't mention his name—
    threatened to kill him,

so he left and never returned.

How did you look and sound and taste to the Alleghwi,
    the Seneca, the Wyandots, the Shawanese, whose paths
    were the only way into and through the forests?

And legend says he was the last one before they
    disappeared altogether.

5. *A Gathering at the River*

Let's stroll down to the river,
wearing the long work
on our hands and faces,

around our eyes, follow
our blood like blackbirds
who call and gather and fill

branches with signals
and silence until suddenly
they are flying the same

direction. Let's cross
the rusted rails, our way lit
by the dipper forming a large

question mark. We'll glare
at the water, a clear black,
its surface reflecting

the freeway's flames that flicker
like the great candelabrum
of the underworld. Earlier,

we walked the streets,
not unnamed, but unmarked,
past the sunken porches,

the "for sale" signs, upward, upward
into where the money lived.
We gazed at the mansions

built with oil and coal, the garrets
and spires, their reward
for turning this all into cash,

every fifth one for sale.
Tires shriek, high-pitched
screams, the air explodes

with the future. Take a coin.
Toss it into the current and wish—
a slight splash, and then the sinking.

The Frackin' Poem

Scarlet tanagers, thrushes, warblers, hawks,
spotted salamanders, skunk and possum,
all the invisible insects—

the native shrubs, the wild flowers,
all the trees cut down, the altered
light patterns, the shifting forest canopy,

all giving way for the gravel roads,
the trucks and tankers and dust,
hauling their chemical cocktails:

the methanol, the isopropyl alcohol,
the ethylene glycon, the crystalline silica,
and all the other toxins, according

to the Halliburton loophole, the industry
refuses to disclose, the toxins that cause
blurry vision, severe stomach cramps,

burning noses, swollen tongues, headaches,
hair loss, ear pressure, horses that won't leave the barn—
smell of sulphur, rotten egg, nail polish,

water burning out of faucets—
the heavy axles invading
across our farms, compacting the topsoil,

reducing plant growth, increasing
the runoff, the erosion like a fully-loaded
cement mixture hauling itself across a lawn

after a heavy rainfall, all the way
to our watersheds: the Ohio, the Susquehanna,
the Delaware, the Erie, the Genesee, the Potomac—

not to mention the 86,000 miles of streams
and rivers, the 161,445 acres of lakes,
the 403,924 acres of wetlands—

the drilling through aquifers, the potential for leakage,
the uranium, the radioactive radon stored
in that black rock that is almost 400 million years old—

that shale that has survived from the Devonian age,
that stone of shelled swimmers, like squids,
of plant-like animals related to starfish called *sea lilies*,

that earth, that earth that once we contaminate
we can never reclaim, that earth
that when we frack, we frack ourselves.

KILLING TIME

Wanting to kill some time between classes,
I drive downtown to return a video.

Late afternoon in late summer,
a few stands setting up for market,

a few stragglers casing out the tomatoes
and corn in the shadow of the library.

I order a strawberry Italian soda
from the café, check out The Ugly Lamp Thrift Store.

Roxanne is at her desk. She looks up.
I have a few minutes to chat,

not a close friend, I ask how
she's doing. *My mother died last week.*

This won't be a quick greeting,
I'm committed, I have to stand here

and say something, I have to console
and I can't look like I'm backing

away, I have to stand like a stone
and speak and ask the expected:

Was she ill? No. Was it sudden?
Yes, and Roxanne is trembling,

she's trying not to show it but
she's burying tears into her cheek,

she's having a small breakdown
and I have to respond,

I have to hold her
and tell her my father died seven

years ago and now we are children
together sobbing and the silence

that follows, and then the small talk, is sweet.

THE BRIDGE

It was about a man pulling the weight
of his drenched body up onto the bridge's hard surface.
It was about a woman whose feet were scarred
by the bridge's gravel so she paused

and stared below into her watery reflection.
A bridge is a road, a wound, one word is a bridge.
The six letters of *bridge* are the six points
of the yellow stars of my ancestors.

Once, we were to meet on the bridge.
We came from our opposite banks
and walked across and married.
Once, my friend balanced on the bridge's edge

arching from the synagogue into the town.
He looked like a rabbi who bridges us and God,
or the Book that bridges God and the rabbi.
He killed himself and became a bridge.

On the roadside I saw the ribcage of a deer
and the legbones that once flighted across the fields
towards my car one evening at sundown, its brown skin
dusky like leaves. I thought it was leaves,

the way they swirl in the wind.
What is a bridge if it crosses into nowhere?
Should we walk out deliberately as if balancing
on swinging planks of wood?

Should we crawl as if through a tunnel into a foreign city?
What if we cross over into barbed wire?
Once, we wondered if we all met in our dreams.
We were curious to know each other

or if we would be strangers until the end of the world.
My mother forgets. Her story is as long
as a bridge would have to be over an ocean.
We were children. We built bridges out of paper

and cards and the letters of our names.
We made bridges out of our bodies.
There is no bridge between then and now.
Or if there is it's a snap of our fingers.

V

So wait with me while I finish my brief visit to space and time.

—Mahmoud Darwish (translated by Fady Joudah)

On This Side of Time

A sparrow clings to the thin branch of the willow.
I know this is another morning of the newspaper
and breakfast and work—nevertheless, we are
at the ready, attentive as the grass is to the wind,
this urging toward completion, examples of the first order,
illustrious, though half of me is distracted, slovenly,
hair tussled, beard unkempt, stained shirt—
can you tell I'm fumbling my way, that I don't know
where I am, let alone where I'm going, in these
intimations of rain, of white apple blossoms blown
across the mustard field, caught up as I am
in the inscrutable meanings of the snapdragons
and the frogs who urge repentance from the dragonflies,
resurrections of my ancestors, herring dealers
      and Talmudic scholars.

      ৯০

Has it gotten through to you by now
that it's all a dream? The volunteer
sunflowers, bowing every-which-way,
the bespeckled apple tree, the evening,
long as it lingers? Will we be among
the stories passed down—not our names,
but something, and so: how do we love
more deeply? How do we grasp
the deeper green sheening of the sweet-
gum leaves? In Moses' farewell speech,
he tells us to choose life and to heed
the commandments, so that we may endure
long upon the soil: *Write down the poem,*
a voice said: *and put it in their mouths.*

❧

Where is that secret part of the soul
where poetry enters, stays its time, leaves?

When your body and soul turn inside out
and your flesh is cold, hot, cold,
your speech incomprehensible,
as if you were speaking a strange language?

And the earth, as it did in the time of Samuel, stands still?

And a voice arises out of a flame,
the one in your heart?

Sometimes it's just a matter
of getting it down right,
of bringing the whole hour
into the poem—

the swallowtail floating its piano key wings across
    the mid-morning sky.

❧

I'm studying to be an expert
of a little sun mixed with a little rain.

Aren't we all specialists?

Or perhaps I'd be the one to consult
about the moon perched
like a fat owl in the sweetgum.

I can write a dissertation,
focusing on when dusk arrives.

Certain silences also suggest themselves.

No way could I achieve the learning
for a higher degree
in how the sudden appearance
of the bluebird affects the heartbeat—

flashes across the garden
and stops it completely.

ॐ

If we can harness
all this loneliness
and longing,
we'd fuel our hearts'
happiness for at least
half a century,
trying even the patience
of God,
who relies
on our losses,
who'd like nothing
better than for us
then to stand up often as we can
and beat our breasts—

ॐ

Now all is quiet save for those sparrows and Neruda
who, too, is blossoming again, the way we all blossom,

even the dead stars, each and every particle of dust
says its testament. Can you read your book while
your eyes survey the earth from end to end? And
when the parchment burns, do the letters float on air?
All I ask is for poetry to stop time, not too difficult
a request, though I know I'm part of a long line
of crazies, of bizarre students of the eternal.
Don't we all want to be loved like King David?
Aren't we all pieces of cloth from the magisterial robe?
And aren't we the ones who cannot distinguish
between the cries of laughter and the cries of weeping?
Can we locate the apocalypse of our lives?

ç

We who would never know if we will know another year,
another day, we who have known and loved those
we can no longer know, or love—here we are, still
partaking of the food and wine, still able to ask
forgiveness, still aching to declare: *I love you,*
and know light from dark, snowfall from silence,
still walking this still-good earth, still learning
that the names of the sages are eclipsed by the names
of their books—we who would trade all the forgotten days
for one remembered hour, we who believe that God
is in the details, that the butterfly koi lazily floating
in the green water is master of the ceremonial moment,
and the morning moon, camouflaged as a clump of cloud—
we who know of beauty to the extent of which we are capable—

ç

so let every question's answer be: *Hummingbird.*

Butterfly bush, sustain me,
hydrangeas release me into the honeysuckle air
of late afternoon silence and the search for shadows,
any shadow, any gathering place
for coolness, any weeping willow
near water, any breeze that would carry the dream forward.

What was it you thought you were doing all those hours
if it wasn't carrying your life along with you?

All those years of silence,
what were they if not some great hesitation
for an ultimate conclusion?

We are arriving envelopes
with time-sensitive materials.

ॐ

Late summer mornings were soft, those days the children
waited for the bus, first days of school and tomatoes piled
into the sink like so many blazing red flowers, the screech
of the blue jay and the cat bounding through the wet meadow.
What is this urge that demands us to translate these moments
into song? I want to write beautiful long lines perfectly realized
as this moment, which doesn't plead or declare its inadequacies,
it only shakes its lush-leaved limbs and bows its school bus yellow
goldenrods and ripples its pond's surface throughout
    the afternoon
into whatever happens next. We want to be a thousand places
    at once,

flying over the harvested garden, the hay collected and baled,
we want the bluebird to suddenly reappear at its feeder the way
it did that morning we sipped coffee and watched our children
     perform
                              backflips on the trampoline.

                    ॐ

It is in this house where we love, here we follow with reverence
the commandments of our one dream and good books.
How over a century ago the wise shaped a clearing
for love of learning and simple beauty and the future.
It will give sustenance to those who praise and celebrate
what the stuff of legends and the visions of the poets foretold.
For travelers it is a place of renewal. Listen
to the bells ringing for you to partake in a ceremony
filled with sacred food and stomping music and
     the continual dance.
Can you hear the joyful laughter in the celestial spheres?
Once there was a story told about a house such as this.
It was made of bread instead of brick and fed a multitude.
Children fell asleep to the soft winds and dreamed
of willows and water. There is no conclusion to the light.

VI

Sing in me, Oh Muse...
—Homer

Writing Through the Dark

I remember how
he'd close himself in
the six-by-six office
in the gray corridor
lined with doors
that mirrored each other
on the seventh story
of the forgotten school
while so many hands in dust-
filled rooms clicked
in unison, one minute
back, two minutes forward
until the ringing ritual
of each hour.

    Past midnight,
no thoughts for sleep,
I'd walk out to nowhere
special, see the single light
illuminating his pane,
think of the hand inside
twitching with ecstasy.

Once, I found the window
he snuck through. Climbing
the flights, I discovered
the crack where the floor
glowed.

    He let me in,
offered me a paper-thin slice
of potato he'd stabbed
onto the end of his blade.

I let the raw moisture
seep on my tongue
as he spoke the poem
until the light in the room
was no longer necessary—

a twig scrapes the glass
and my small study
is in the black window:
chimes, lamp, page, face,
this slow sliding into dawn.

Two for Uncle Walt

1. Whitman Alone

Imagine: there he is—
walking, one hand holding
the other, a solitary

late afternoon stroll,
crossing and re-crossing
the streets, swaying down

to the river, humming
an aria as the ferry lifts
him over the water

to the city of his poem
and back again, conferring
with the conductor, the smell

of fish and salt and sweat
from the workers who rush
home as the six bells warn:

the dark is here, go
warm yourselves, not one
knowing or caring to know

the tall hefty bearded son
with the cocked back hat
and the hysterical eyes

who stumbles along walkways
and mumbles to himself,
laughing his fool head off.

Watch him awhile,
around and around the wharf,
glancing at sailors, pissing

against the side of buildings—
it almost justifies this moment
as the dark comes on

and the neighborhood shuts
its windows to the chill
and wind in bare branches,

crows gawking crazily
and he out there
looking up at the stars

and scratching his chin—
it makes sense, imagine—
the whole of us are in the balance.

2. *Whitman's Voice*

Center of equal daughters, equal sons, all, grown, ungrown, all, all alike
endear'd, grown, young or old, Strong, ample, fair, enduring, capable,
rich, Perennial with the Earth, with Freedom, Law and Love...

In the indecisive weather of March
we talk— over coffee and particles
of afternoon dust that could be souls,
dishes clattering, a siren's wail,
the radio with its distinct muttering—
about our poetry and its difficulties,
how they say we can't write anymore
about love and suddenly the radio guy
announces the discovery of Whitman's
voice, and we turn our heads, strain

our ears, the crackle and the creak
of the soft Brooklyn accent sounding
the primitive words into the primitive
recorder, one experiment speaking
into another, barely audible the way
it was to the aristocratic citizens
who heard only what they expected
and not the hairiness of a sprawling
urgency. A chill suspends us
to the barely comprehensible, this sage,
this father, this name and face and song
that sang our country, and wept,
sings to us now, here, in Cleveland,
and we turn back to our poetry not the same.

To You, Sylvia

Thank you, Sylvia S. Vogal—whoever you were,
you and I have much in common—specifically,

this book of thatched cardboard cover, binding
a bit loose but holding together, that I discovered

one off-day scrounging through the barn loft—
Whitman's book, your name and date:

Sylvia S. Vogel, September 1940 scribbled beneath
"Selected and Edited by one Christian Murley

and illustrated by Lewis C. Daniel,
copyright MCMX." And it occurs to me

it's September now, 83 years later—perhaps
you're in the graveyard across from the very barn

I found you in—yes, Sylvia, you, because
who are we if not the books we read?

And if Whitman isn't part of you and me,
we haven't really read him, have we?

And when I opened the thick volume, pages
intact and just a bit stained by time, it was

"To You," the poem I mean, which I hadn't
read before, and so I read it now, Sylvia, to you:

"Whoever you are," it begins, "your true soul
and body appear before me...I place my hand

upon you, that you be my poem, I whisper
with my lips close to your ear, I've loved

many women and men, but I love not better
than you," dear Sylvia S. Vogal of September,

1940, who left this book for me to find in September,
2023, in a barn across from the graveyard where, perhaps,

you are, and perhaps I'll be, reading, together,
this illustrated edition of *Leaves of Grass*.

LETTER TO WRIGHT AFTER VISITING HIS GRAVE

Robert and I abandon the iPhone's directions
to drive north up Route 9 and instead
follow the scrawled notes your beloved Annie

gave Robert: *take the Cross Bronx,*
get off at Jerome Avenue, merge with traffic
under the rattling elevated. "My territory,"

Robert says and point to the vacant lot
that was his childhood home. We weave
our way to the Burden plot, an irony

you surely would appreciate, so many
of your years a burden, from Martin's Ferry
to the Institution until your late love lifted you

across the dark waters to the lizards
and statues of Apollo and lightning bugs
in the afternoon, one of those poems

from your work we read back and forth
above what remains of your body.
Two scholars, we discuss, even debate,

that famous last line about wasting
your life: was it referring to the failure
you concluded you had come to?

Or, rather, did you finally give yourself up
to the present moment? Over forty years ago
you advised us not to worry over the dead,

so we turn toward your stone, shadowed
by the cherry tree's unseasonable pink blossoms
and read, inevitably, your blessings.

READING PHILIP LEVINE

(1928-2015)

The last person to read this book
was Molly Renee Miller of 7527 Drive,
San Antonio Texas, 78249-2518, United
States of America. I know this
because the receipt is between pages
40 and 41, and she paid $8.95 on
December 30, 2011, at 8:41 P.M.
And now here it is, at 620 12th Street,
Franklin, Pennsylvania 4:17 A.M,
and of course I'm wondering
what you thought about it, Molly,
if you read it all the way through,
if it moved you as it's moved me
with its descriptions of the poet's
early days reading Dostoevsky and
lying beside his brother, as I did,
in that corner room down the hall
from our parents, how my brother
and I played twenty questions until
one of us fell asleep dreaming of animals,
vegetables and minerals. If you used this receipt
as a bookmark, you might have read
the earlier poem about the two workers
who didn't know each other well but the man
interpreted the woman's greased-stained lifeline
and she spit on his dirty glasses and
dried them with a napkin as they talked
until the bar closed and they parted
and walked home by themselves
but changed in ways they themselves
didn't understand. Did that poem move you
as it moved me? To consider how most

of who we are consists of what we'll never
understand, the way the poet won't
reveal what happened between those two,
whether they will never meet again
or they will fall in love and grow old
and the man will write the poem about
the lucky life he's lived, as I hope
your life is, Molly Renee Miller,
fellow-reader of this one book
that passed from your hands to mine.
I wonder, as I do now, if you set the book aside
and walked out at 5 A.M in the negative
six-degree 25 mile-an-hour wind chill
to look at the crescent moon,
because we've been reading a poet
who passed this very night, because
the wide Main Street will never
be more empty, because—
how could we know it at the time?—
we now realize that when a poet
who has come to live inside us
has taken leave of this earth,
we have no other option but
to wake and face the beautiful
cold emptiness and stroll the silent
streets until the only sound is
our hearts, beating in time
with all the words he left inside us.

ILYA'S VOICE

for Ilya Kaminsky

All of his person contained in each stress—
cries, flays, leaps, soars, sinks, hovers,

his throat, his breath, his blood,
strict to each syllable, scratch, scar,

pleads, invokes, pronounces—
the room cannot contain such a voice,

nor a house, a temple, a sky,
each accented wail, stretching,

the pain primal, animal, the occasional sweet sad love, tender,
infused in the anguish, the centuries—

then the silence, deafening.

Letter to Roche from Clarksburg, West Virginia

Dear Dan: Well, I haven't even made it to Charleston, yet,
and at this rate the store your friends Mike and Nancy own
that sells exotic artsy *tchotchkes* like Peruvian blankets
and Sumerian beads will be closed. And it will be dark,

and I'll park the car and be greeted by the one prostitute
who walks the same blocks over and over. She'll ask
in her black strapless shirt and shorts what my pleasure is
and I'll say something local to eat and she'll point me

down toward the river where the only restaurant open
will serve chicken and dumplings, the torn newspaper
at the counter no extra charge. I'll proceed to the river
and try to recall when my first wife and I visited you

when you lived with your first wife and that old German
Shepherd Grits who didn't belong to anyone
in that big farm house and hundred acres
you rented and made lentil soup and baked bread

and then the two of us walked the railroad tracks,
Grits following, talking about our writing, in other words,
our lives, what we still talk about, so nothing has changed
except now we are stunned because each of us fooled

another woman to fall in love with us, each of us found
a second chance with luck and a refusal to give in. Maybe
it's because we exist to remind each other of towns
like these—Clarksburg and Charleston and Ames, Iowa

and Knoxville, Tennessee and Oil City, Pennsylvania—
empty downtowns and real diners and unswept floors,
not the kind they make up to look like diners, with fresh
painted walls and posters of Dean and Brando, but

diners where we've sat for hours over bad coffee
and something local, like "the Derrick special" or
a burger so large it would for a while shut us up.
Because we had the world to talk about, what with

how we wanted to infuse each of our moments
with some magic, so that meant being honest with our lives—
the failures and the fortunes, the joys and embarrassments.
Somehow we kept in touch. And that's a kind of miracle.

Friendship is what wears more comfortable with the years,
and also keeping faith in one of those original ideals.
It somehow survives the occasional antagonisms
that are part and parcel of anything alive and human.

Our on-going debate between poetry and prose, for example,
how our passion for our own discipline almost killed us,
not you and I, personally, but us, and we learned
how thin the line really is between friends and enemies,

and that any friendship, no matter how long lasting,
is a public act, and the ancient formalities forged over the ages
still hold up the lightness of all our spontaneous gestures.
Everyone knows poetry is the higher art, dummy, and I say this

with the greatest love. You'll write an essay proving me wrong,
and on it will go, because this is the most prosaic poem
I've ever written. Your influence? Maybe. This life-long
companionship is work, my man: it means higher phone bills

and filling each other in on the details of our lives
and that means trust, after all, the one thing we writers
mostly fail at, given that anything goes, we'd rip out the hearts
of our own mothers for a good publication, wouldn't we? Some.

Remember that night in Columbus, the Blue Danube,
we were drinking imported beer and eating Greek Salad
and told ourselves we were writers, and believed it,
and we couldn't be posing because we were already past

the stage of trying to impress each other. Then
you paid the check, or I did, and we went back home
to our own lonely work which, when the time came,
we'd read to each other, poem and essay, offering up

to the other that which was most essential.

ZORBATIC

for Scott Minar

Hoch funf! we'd shout, *auf Deutsh*, or at least
in the sophomoric language we were learning,
and we'd raise our right hands into the air as if
pledging allegiance and slap them hard and solid.
Strange affection, this ache of palms.
But in those Zorbatic years our love of life
was lyrical and sometimes we sang to each other,
the way we wished our respective older brothers
would do, just once, in German: *hoch funf!*
hoch zehn! hock kupf! and we'd butt our craniums
like two bulls cracking up at the nonsense.
We cut class, pitched pennies—you and Curt
and Keith and Kevin and I, shooting pool at Swanky's,
where you'd profess: *Be the ball!*, your mantra
playing hoops where you'd rarely miss,
your needle's eye swishing the net, and so we assumed
the ball was you. Athens, Ohio, our twenties,
Casa Que Pasa for late breakfast, afternoons long
and walking the rails beyond the lumber mill,
sitting on the trestle where you swore that if
you owned the world everyone would dance
around naked. Nights drinking the Union
Bar and Grill out of their supply of Tequila.
Once, we went to the cemetery behind
the state mental health hospital and stared
silently at the stones with numbers for names,
arranged in a circle. You prostrated yourself
to no authority we could hear, your muscular body
bowed low, your lips kissing the wet ground,
your way of honoring the moment.
You were the king of our charmed town,
our little Hollywood of Ohio, in your 1940's

gentleman suit, huge and handsome and skilled,
singing in your sweet voice the song about
the boy's suicide: *I'm holding out my only candle,*
with so little light to find my way...
One freezing night, close to dawn, my face
taking shape in the window above what few words
I managed to scratch on the open page,
you appeared with the poem that demonstrated
conclusively that you had, during its moments
of composure, become whatever it was
that called it forth, a lesser star, visible and
affirming its small space in the enormous sky.
It doesn't have a name, the poem says,
and we walked those hilly streets, the season's
first snow surprising the air, toward the river,
into the future, this moment.

Our Mothers Have the Same Name

for David Citino (1947-2005)

Great teacher, what you revealed in your office
after you closed the door and looked into my eyes
was your illness. I was your student and ignorant

of the weight of a life. Something about your brain
and spinal cord and signals and scar tissue,
your nerves confused like this snow that blizzards

out of all proportion to itself, scattering the leaves
and pursuing the dry stubble. Under a circle of light,
I'm reading *The Book of Job*: none like him

in all the earth, the way each flake of this whiteout
continues to amaze, so many and none the same,
the treasures we enter and know our portion

is worth more than gold or jewels or what
can be measured, the countless minutia,
our daily ecstasies, the saints and sages

of every second and place, even Columbus,
Ohio, where your angel landed, strolling
with your cane in the center of the state,

Whitman of the malls, jester of White Castle,
chanting this capital city and its citizens of chain stores
and the Big Ten into a song of higher physics

that insists that they are beautiful and resolves,
the way three yards and a cloud of dust
becomes for you the stuff of apocrypha, in God.

You charm magic out of engineering majors
and football players in rhythm and alliteration, lifting us
at least for a semester outside of ourselves.

We know you are the nun your poems keep referring to,
the Sister who soaks up the world with the sponge
of her Catholic soul. After class, we'd watch you,

face flushed with the music of the spheres,
limping the five stories to your service on the top floor,
in the higher reaches, the office where you instruct

so many and strengthen the weak hands,
all of us students, you'd say, of holy assignments,
the most recent incarnations of the first explosion.

We knew, as you shuffled a few inches above
the hallway, in the rarified air, that you were composing
another poem in your head. Even while making pasta

the Muse is always with you, her favored son,
the John Donne of the Midwest, all sermons and sex.
Once, Friday night on the empty campus, I climbed

the flights toward the clamor and the light
splashing from the crack beneath your floor—
scotch and cigars with the saints, Saint Francis

and Einstein, Woody Hayes and the Trickster,
the Virgin and Rocky Colavito, Mario Lanza
dueling your father in a battle of "Volare."

Even your Italian grandfather was shaking
his olive tree he brought all the way from Calabria.
And you didn't forget to invite the lonely and lost

whose names you curried from the Personals
in your continual party celebrating everything.
Above your desk the words: *Speak Slowly.*

It wasn't so much the poetry you taught me.
It was the quotidian, and how each word is a bird
of intention. Hath the rain a father?

Where were we during the foundations?
And how it is all a-flowering.
And how the exhaustion is a breakdown

of a body that cannot hold such Leviathan
of spirit, David, like the theory of the expanding
universe, each and every exploding star.

MEETING THE SWAMI

for Joshua Cappy and Rick Steigerwald

I looked into the swami's face.
It was a slow burning fire.

"Throw your karma in my basket," it said.

It was like the garden,
early summer evening,
asking us to sit beside it,
to look closely into it.

Stay and admire me,
now that you are more fully awake.

      ❧

But isn't there only one God
who cannot be seen, or named—

no flesh, no robe, no incense,
no raga, no dharma,

no private plane, no ashrams,
no holy water

dripped into the hands
of the devotees

waiting in long lines
to look into your holy face?

Only this dusk and fireflies,
these white Madonna lilies,

this dark now descending
and the birdsong?

࿒

Yet I looked into the swami's face.
It was red and blissful.
I came from somewhere else.
But in that moment, in that short moment,
I was blissful, too.

࿒

There's a white peacock
where the swami is,
strutting wherever it wants—

I watch it linger,

until I arrive back to its source, to India,
or to that place where white
was created.

࿒

There are a thousand pairs of shoes
in front of the open gate
the raagas chant through.

࿒

I have been responsible for many deaths,
and I fear karma will not be kind to me.
But let us try to emerge from that sadness,
like the bird escaping the netted blueberry bush, and singing.

৯

On an evening like this,
one doesn't know where to start, or finish.

My Blossoming Everything

for Ganya

It is robins' eggs on the just out-of-reach branch.
It is red raspberries in a circular thicket of thorns.
Who are you, my beloved? My sweetness,
My swallowtail, my infinite youth?
My pine shadow in the tall grass?
My other self, unreachable, my untrappable hummingbird,
My synagogue empty of all but God, my scripture
upon which I write my illegible inheritance,
My last night's dream that woke me in confusion,
My wings removed in my mother's womb,
My knowledge emptying with my age, my words
The silence will send out to the silence,
My light I cup in my hands and splash on my face,
My Jupiter newly risen like my heart?

When You Are Older

you might recall this café in Grove City,
Pennsylvania, waiting for your daughter
riding Rusty at her horseback lesson—
you sipped latte in a large mug and read
the work of an ancient poet, listening
to the rain on the slate, all alone, and happy.
When you are old this will be another day
blurred in a lifetime of days, a day you wrote:
I love this life, but how can I translate
that love into words? A day you compared
your wife to one of those slender Madonna lilies
blossoming in her garden. A day you read:
Let the moment expand until time reveal its illusion,
the illusion of this day, the day you wrote this, remember?

To Sing, Sweetly, Forever

How each moment reveals our resurrection,
and to wonder what or who allowed us to witness

this fog dispersing, this water, this flower,
is to wonder why the mourning dove

would look back to the branch from
which it sprang into flight, with so much

sky ahead, or to speculate on how
a tree's shadow is devoted to the tree,

until dark descends and they both
disappear into a larger devotion,

that place behind the ribs, where
we carry each person we love

for the rest of our lives. And now
the white lily is drenched by rain

that woke us into love, how
the world happens, by happenstance

or design, and that the candle burning
all night and into the morning burns

doubled in the window. So let us
fill our souls with beauty, and truth,

and how as the soul came in it goes forth
a life fully lived, like a bird entering

through a window and leaving
through another window,

and that our lives are an allowance
for that soul to sing, sweetly, forever.

NOTES AND LINKS

Page 69. "Where the Ducks Walk on the Fish" (The Spillway in Linesville, PA),
https://visitcrawford.org/listing/pymatuning-spillway/

"River of Many Names" (formally titled "Our Rivers, Our Lives") was performed as the libretto as a celebration on the 125th anniversary of Clarion University, composition by Jaropolk Lassowsky

Page 124. "Whitman's Voice" may be heard here:
https://www.youtube.com/watch?v=cnMoUm87QII

"To Sing, Sweetly, Forever" was used as the text to a composition for voice, alto flute, and piano by Brent Register and was published by Alry Productions.

A performance of "To Sing, Sweetly, Forever" can be found here:
https://soundcloud.com/alrypublications/p-brent-register-to-sing-sweetly-forever-for-voice-alto-flute-and-piano

ACKNOWLEDGEMENTS

Along These Rivers: Poetry and Photography from Pittsburgh: "Lost Dog"

North American Review: "The Rabbi of Box Turtles," "The FlyingSquirrels"

The Connecticut Review: "My Brother and I Holding Hands"

Fourth River: "Willie Wheeler," "Under the Flyway"

In Pittsburgh: "This Magnitude"

Lake Effect: "A Million Angels Falling"

Larry's Poetry Review: "What Dorothy Knew"

The Laurel Review: "On This Side of Time"

Mad Swirl: "Whitman Alone"

Magazine 1: "Killing Time"

The Nebraska Review: "Swallows"

Nine Mile Art and Lit Magazine: "At Camp Wise" (as "Grackles"), "Turning 60," "Spring Chronicle," "The Mourner" (as "This Crazy Devotion"), "For You, Sylvia"

The North American Review: "My Blossoming Everything," "The Bridge"

Pittsburgh Post-Gazette: "When You Are Old"

The Pittsburgh Quarterly Review: "Walking," "We Mourners"

Poetry.com: "Appointment with the Peacocks"

Poetry International: "4000" (as "14, 000")

Terrain.org: "A Poetry as Perfect as a June Morning"

Vox Populi: "Reading Philip Levine," "Meeting the Swami"

The Watershed Journal: "Working Through the Dark,"
   "Small Beautiful Thing"

Written on Water: Writings About the Allegheny River:
   "River of Many Names"

To my blossoming everyones, too numerous to mention who, through their generosity, kindness, and wisdom, help me to become a better human being, including: Chris Hood, Mimi Terman, Bella Terman, Scott Minar, David Swerdlow, Rick St. John, Jane McCafferty, Patrick Tierney, Lori Jakiela, Al Maginnes, Ann Pancake, John Miller, Saleh Razzouk, Dan Roche, Judy Rock, Mike Simms, James and Lynn Stewart, David Terman, Stuart Terman, Susan Terman, Tony Vallone, Ben Vincent, Cantor Michal Grey-Shaffer, The Bridge Literary Center Team, Marc Nieson, Marty Meyer, Tom Doerr, The Hoods, Marty Forchheimer, Brian Engel, Steve Kuusisto, Yehoshua November, Baruch November.

Infinite gratitude to Ruth Thompson and Don Mitchell for their inspiration and friendship.

Philip Terman's books include *This Crazy Devotion* (Broadstone), *Our Portion: New and Selected Poems* (Autumn House) and, as co-translator,  *Tango Beneath a Narrow Ceiling: The Selected poems of Riad Saleh Hussein* (Bitter Oleander). Forthcoming is *The Whole Mishpocha: New and Selected Jewish Poems* (BenYehuda Press). A selection of his poems, *My Dear Friend Kafka* (Nimwa Press, Damascus) was translated into Arabic by Saleh Razzouk.

His poems and essays appear in many journals and anthologies, such as *Poetry Magazine, The Kenyon Review, Poetry International, The Sun, The Bloomsbury Anthology of Contemporary Jewish Poetry,* and *Extraordinary Rendition: American Writers on Palestine.*

He directs The Bridge Literary Arts Center, a regional writer's organization in western, PA , conducts poetry workshops and coaches writing hither and yon. philipterman.my.canva.site

www.ingramcontent.com/pod-product-compliance
Lightning Source LLC
Chambersburg PA
CBHW020357130626
46549CB00006B/2313